Young Frederick Douglass

FIGHT FOR FREEDOM

Young Frederick Douglass

FIGHT FOR FREEDOM

by Laurence Santrey
illustrated by Bert Dodson

Troll Associates

Library of Congress Cataloging in Publication Data

Santrey, Laurence.
    Young Frederick Douglass, fight for freedom.

    Summary: Presents the early life of the slave who
became an abolitionist, journalist, and statesman.
    1. Douglass, Frederick, 1817?-1895—Juvenile litera-
ture.   2. Abolitionists—United States—Biography—
Juvenile literature.   3. Afro-Americans—Biography—
Juvenile literature.   [1. Douglass, Frederick, 1817?-
1895.   2. Afro-Americans—Biography]   I. Dodson, Bert,
ill.   II. Title.
E449.D75S26   1983   973.8′092′4   [B]   [92]   82-15993
ISBN 0-89375-857-4
ISBN 0-89375-858-2 (pbk.)

10   9   8   7   6   5   4   3   2

Young Frederick Douglass

FIGHT FOR FREEDOM

Fred Baily's world was bleak and poor. The little boy didn't know it, though, for Betsey and Isaac Baily, his grandparents, were kind and loving people. They took good care of Fred and his young cousins.

7

The children lived with Grandmama and Grandpapa because their mothers were not allowed to keep them. Their mothers— Grandmama Baily's daughters—were slaves who worked on different plantations on the eastern shore of Maryland. When one of them had a baby, Grandmama Baily took it in. She raised the child until it was old enough to be put to work by its slave owner.

Fred, who was born about 1817, was better off than a lot of other slave children. Many of them had no relatives like Grandmama Baily to care for them. Those children were raised by strangers, who did not treat them well. But Fred's grandmother made sure that her little ones had enough food and plenty of affection, and that they never felt lonely or frightened.

Betsey Baily was smart and skilled in many ways. One of her special talents was farming. Her sweet potatoes grew bigger and better—and there were more of them—than anyone else's in the whole area. The neighbors said she was "born to good luck." But, as Fred wrote years later, Grandmama's secret wasn't luck. It was the special care and attention she gave to her seedlings.

To keep her sweet-potato seedlings from being destroyed by frost, she actually buried the roots under the hearth of her cabin during the winter months. Then, when they were planted, they were healthy and grew well. Whenever the neighbors had seedlings to put in the ground, they sent for Grandmama Betsey. "If she but touches them at planting," the neighbors believed, "they will be sure to grow and flourish." For lending her magic touch, Mrs. Baily was always given a share of the crop. And that brought more food into the Baily cabin.

For the first few years of his life, Fred never saw his mother. He didn't even *know* what a mother was. As for his father—the idea of such a person never entered his mind. If Fred belonged to anyone, it was to his master.

Little Fred spent his days playing with his cousins, helping his grandmother, or fishing in the river near the cabin. His only clothing was a rough, knee-length shirt. A slave child was given two shirts each year. Even if these shirts were torn or lost, there were no new ones until the year was up. Long after, Fred remembered, "In the hottest summer and the coldest winter, I was kept almost naked. No shoes, no stockings, no jacket, no trousers. Nothing but the coarse shirt reaching down to my knees. This I wore night and day, changing it once a week."

Until he was around five years old, Fred didn't know he was a slave. Then he heard his grandparents talking about the "Old Master," who owned all of Fred's family. There was a sad note in Grandmama Betsey's voice when she spoke about the plantation, where Fred would soon have to go. The little boy didn't understand much of what they were saying, but the sound of it made him shiver.

Nothing happened for two years. Then, one summer morning, Betsey Baily took her grandson's hand and set off along the road. She didn't tell him where they were going, or why. She didn't cry or show any of the gloom she was feeling. Not once on the twelve-mile walk to the plantation house did she speak one sad word. Yet somehow, Fred sensed that something terrible was happening.

15

In the blazing afternoon heat, Mrs. Baily and Fred reached the plantation. The little boy saw many houses, farm animals, men, women, and children. All of this stunned him. Living at Grandmama's, he had never seen so many buildings and people all in one place.

Mrs. Baily brought Fred over to a young boy and two young girls. "Fred," she said, "here is your brother, Perry. And these are your sisters, Sarah and Eliza. You run along and play with them. I'll sit in the kitchen and visit awhile."

Fred was confused and trembling. The children

might be called brother and sisters, but they were strangers to him. He clung tightly to Grandmama's skirt. He wanted to go home.

Grandmama insisted that Fred stay outside and play. She gave him a gentle push toward the other children. Then she walked away. Fred stood there, watching the other children play. Time passed, but he didn't budge from the spot. Then a child ran over to him, saying, "Your grand-mammy's gone." Fred couldn't believe it. He dashed into the house to see for himself. It *was* true! Grandmama Betsey was gone.

The heart-broken boy threw himself on the floor and sobbed. His brother and sisters tried to comfort him, but nothing could stop his tears. Fred felt betrayed, terrified, and all alone. Now he suddenly understood what his grandparents had been talking about and why they had been so sad. Lying on the dirt floor, Fred cried himself to sleep.

For the next two years, Fred lived on the plantation as the slave of a man named Captain Anthony. Fred was still too young to work in the fields, so he was given other chores. He helped the older boys bring in the cows for milking. He kept the front yard clean. He ran errands for Captain Anthony's family.

Even though the work wasn't too difficult, Fred was always hungry and tired. Slaves were awakened long before sunrise and kept busy until long after dark. Breakfast for the slave children was cornmeal mush. It was dumped into a large wooden bowl on the ground. All the children squatted around the bowl to eat, scooping up the mush with oyster shells, flat stones, or their fingers.

The strongest children and the fastest eaters got the most food. But *nobody* ever had enough food. Little Fred got the least of all because Aunt Katy, the cook, was his enemy.

One morning, Katy threatened to starve the life out of Fred. All day, he tried to keep up his spirits, hoping she would forget by dinnertime. But she didn't. At sundown, she gave each of the children dinner—one slice of corn bread. When Fred reached for his, she pulled away the loaf and sent him out of the kitchen.

The eight-year-old boy, too hungry to fall asleep that night, was sitting outside the kitchen door when he had a surprise visitor. It was his mother. Harriet Baily was almost a stranger to Fred. Since he had come to the plantation, he had seen her only three times.

Fred's mother was a slave on a farm fifteen miles away. The only way she could visit her children was to walk thirty miles at night. Her long, hard day in the fields left her too tired for that kind of walk. This time, however, she was able to get a ride on a cart.

Harriet Baily put her arm around Fred and asked him how he was. He told her he was hungry and that the cook had threatened to starve him to death. The woman kissed her son, stroked his cheek, and said, "I won't let anyone starve you!" Then she gave him a heart-shaped ginger cake coated with sugar.

As soon as Fred finished the last crumb, his mother took him into the kitchen. In a voice filled with fury, she told Aunt Katy, "You're a slave just like the rest of us. How can you do these things to a harmless little child?"

Harriet Baily's angry words didn't change Katy's treatment of Fred. But his mother's visit still made a big difference in the young boy's life. "That night," he remembered, "I learned that I was not only a child, but *somebody's* child." He knew that his mother loved him very much, and even though she couldn't be with him, she thought of him all the time. But after that night, Fred never saw Harriet Baily again. She died when Fred was only eight or nine years old.

Before he was ten years old, Fred was sent to the city of Baltimore. He was going to work for Sophia and Hugh Auld, relatives of Captain Anthony. The young boy was glad to leave the plantation. He felt that whatever lay ahead could not be worse.

On a sunny Saturday morning in spring, Fred
was dressed in a clean shirt and his first pair of
pants. He was put aboard a sloop bound for
Baltimore—a trip he never forgot. He gaped at the
broad Chesapeake Bay and all the boats sailing on
it. He marveled at the town of Annapolis, with its

beautiful houses and the great shining dome of the State House. But most exciting of all was Baltimore itself, a city teeming with life. For the youngster who had never been away from the country, this was a fantasyland.

One of the sailors took Fred to the Auld house. Fred was met at the door by Mr. and Mrs. Auld and their little son, Tommy. Fred knew he was going to live with them and take care of Tommy. He didn't know how he was going to be treated. But when little Tommy smiled and took his hand, the young slave could see that fate had been kind to him.

Instead of sleeping on the ground, Fred now slept indoors on a bed of straw. He had clean clothes and enough food to fill his belly. Nobody beat him, and Mrs. Auld treated him like an ordinary child instead of a slave.

Every afternoon, when Fred brought Tommy home from play, the boys joined Mrs. Auld in the front parlor. There they sat quietly, listening to her read from the Bible.

Fred loved to hear Mrs. Auld read aloud. He enjoyed the sounds of the words and the wonderful stories they made. He wished he could read them, too. And so, one day, he asked Mrs. Auld if she would teach him to read. "Why, how nice, Fred," she said. "It's delightful that you want to read the Bible. Of course, I'll teach you. We shall start with the alphabet this very afternoon!"

In the days that followed, Mrs. Auld gave Fred a reading lesson every afternoon. Soon the young slave knew the alphabet and could spell many short words. Fred looked forward to each afternoon's lesson with great excitement and was very proud when Mrs. Auld praised him for being so bright. He had never known such joy.

One evening, Mrs. Auld told her husband how well Fred was learning to read. Mr. Auld scowled. "You must stop these lessons right now!" he told his wife. "Don't you know that it is against the law to teach slaves to read? It's a bad thing to do."

"I didn't know it was against the law," Mrs. Auld answered. "And I cannot understand why it would be bad for a slave to read."

"A slave should know nothing but the will of his master," Mr. Auld explained. "If you teach that boy how to read, he'll be forever unfit for the duties of a slave. The knowledge will do him no good, and it will do us a great deal of harm."

Mrs. Auld never gave Fred another lesson. In fact, she did everything possible to stop him from learning. If she saw the boy looking at a newspaper or book, she snatched it away. And if she didn't see or hear him doing some task, she accused him of sneaking off somewhere to read.

Life changed for Mrs. Auld, too. She was obeying the law and her husband. She was being a good slave owner. But she was no longer a happy woman.

Fred was hurt deeply by what had happened, but he learned two valuable lessons. First, he realized that his owners wanted him to be a slave forever. He understood now that people were not slaves because of something they did. They were slaves because somebody else wanted them to be.

The second lesson was that the way out of slavery was through knowledge. That was why slave owners kept their slaves ignorant. Once slaves could read road signs, they might run away from their masters. Once they found out that there were states without slavery, they might try to reach them. Once they learned to write, they could forge the papers slaves needed to travel. And once they could count, they could use money to buy train tickets and food.

Young Fred Baily made up his mind to learn how to read and write. First, he read everything he could from a spelling book someone had thrown away. Whenever he came to a word he didn't know, he made a small mark under it and asked one of the neighborhood children to tell him what it was. Fred paid for these brief lessons with cookies from the Auld kitchen. By the time he was thirteen, Fred could read very well.

About the same time, Fred began working in the shipyard owned by Mr. Auld. His job was to clean up, watch the yard when nobody else was around, and keep the office fire going. There were many hours when he was alone, and Fred used them to teach himself to write.

One day, he found a school notebook Tommy Auld had finished using. In the spaces between the lines, Fred copied Tommy's writing. He worked in the kitchen by firelight, waiting until the Auld family was fast asleep.

Then in March 1833, Fred was sent back to the plantation. There was a big argument in the Auld family between Hugh Auld and his brother, Thomas. As a result, Hugh had to return Fred to the country.

Thomas Auld, Fred's new master, treated his slaves badly. Yet, no matter how many hardships he had to endure, Fred refused to beg or weep or show any other sign that it bothered him. This made Thomas Auld so furious that he sent Fred away to be "broken."

On January 1, 1834, Fred was brought to the farm of Edward Covey. For a fee, Covey promised that he would turn "trouble-making" slaves into obedient workers.

For the first six months, Fred took everything Covey handed out. But one day, when Covey was beating Fred, the seventeen-year-old slave fought back. Fred won the fight, knocking Covey to the ground. The enraged slave breaker swore he would kill Fred. But the teenager knew better. Covey would not do anything that would cost him his fee.

From that moment until Fred left Covey's, the young slave was never whipped, nor did Covey ever again challenge him. Years later, Fred wrote, "This battle with Mr. Covey was the turning point in my life as a slave. It rekindled in me the smoldering embers of liberty. I was a changed being after that fight. I was *nothing* before; *I was a man now.* It inspired me with a renewed determination to be *a free man!*"

After three years of farm work in the country, Fred was sent back to Baltimore. There, Hugh Auld got him a job in a friend's shipyard. Fred liked the work—he was a skilled laborer now—and he was happier in Baltimore than he had been in the country. But there was one important thing still missing—his freedom! Then he met a man who offered him a way to escape slavery.

The man was a black sailor who had seaman's papers. These papers, issued by the United States government, proved that the sailor was not a slave. With them, he was free to travel anywhere in the country. The sailor offered to lend Fred his papers. "Put these in your pocket," he said, "and you can go North to freedom. You can mail them back to me when you're safe in New York or Boston."

On September 3, 1838, wearing sailor's clothing and carrying his friend's papers, Fred Baily got on a northbound train. He didn't stop until he reached New Bedford, Massachusetts, a ship-building town. There, Fred took a job in a shipyard, married Anna Murray, a free black woman from Baltimore, and started a new life.

It was in New Bedford that Fred took the last name of Douglass. As Fred Baily, he might be traced by bounty hunters who were paid for turning in runaway slaves. With a new name, Frederick Douglass, he had a much better chance of staying free.

It was also in New Bedford that Fred began the career that would make him world famous. He started by joining a group of abolitionists, people devoted to ending slavery. He read everything he could about slavery and listened to the leading abolitionists of his day. Then, in 1841, Frederick Douglass made his first anti-slavery speech. It thrilled his audience, and it brought him to the attention of every important person in the abolitionist movement.

For the next four years, Frederick Douglass toured the Northern states, speaking against slavery. He also wrote the story of his life. The book, which described his years as a slave, was read all over the United States. It was even read by the Auld family, who grew very angry. They went to court to have their runaway slave returned to them.

43

Douglass's friends were afraid that he would be arrested and sent back to Maryland, so they put him on a ship bound for England. He stayed in England for two years and became a very popular speaker and writer. But he wanted to come home, where he felt a strong voice against slavery was needed more than ever. To make this possible, his friends raised enough money to buy Douglass's freedom from the Aulds.

When he returned to the United States in the years before the Civil War, Frederick Douglass continued his work for freedom. He started a weekly newspaper in Rochester, New York called *The North Star.* This paper soon became a leading force in the battle against slavery.

Shortly after the war began, Douglass went to see President Abraham Lincoln. He urged the President to recruit black men, as well as white, into the Union Army.

"Why do you fight the rebels with only one hand," Douglass asked, "when you might strike effectively with two?"

Lincoln agreed. Within months, thousands of black men were fighting for the Union. Among them were two of Frederick Douglass's sons.

Even though the Civil War ended slavery, many problems remained for black people. They still did not have equal rights. In many places, they could not vote, hold public office, find jobs, or get an education. And so, Douglass continued his battle for civil rights and freedom. He fought tirelessly for an end to job discrimination and to the segregation in schools and places of worship.

Frederick Douglass did not stop fighting until his death on February 20, 1895. Yet, even though he is gone, his beliefs are still alive today. Douglass's words continue to live, showing others the path to freedom and equality for *all* people.